NATURE'S GOT TALENT

SUPERSTAR MAMMALS

Louise Spilsbury

PowerKiDS press™

New York

Published in 2015 by The Rosen Publishing Group
29 East 21st Street, New York, NY 10010

Produced for Rosen by Calcium Creative Ltd
Editor for Calcium Creative Ltd: Sarah Eason
US Editor: Joshua Shadowens
Designer: Paul Myerscough

Photo credits: Cover: Shutterstock: Eric Isselee (top), Efired (left), FineShine (right); Inside:
Dreamstime: Michael Elliott 15l, Alexandre Fagundes De Fagundes 18l, Karelgallas 18r,
Mr1805 26; Flickr: R. G. Daniel 14r; Getty Images: Hiroya Minakuchi 27tl; National
Science Foundation: Kyle Hoppe 27br; Shutterstock: Henk Bentlage 1, 20, 21l, 21r,
Kim Briers 11br, Heather M Davidson 23tl, Dennis Donohue 12, 13tl, Aubord Dulac
14l, EBFoto 17, Efired 9bl, Fotokon 22, Haveseen 8, 9tr, Eric Isselee 2–3, 16, 19,
24, Tao Jiang 25tr, Gail Johnson 29br, Jeannette Katzir Photog 13br, Christian Musat
11tl, Steve Noakes 10, Nagel Photography 4, Stuart G Porter 6–7, Redswept 29tl, Tom
Reichner 28, Bernhard Richter 25bl, Alan Scheer 7, Joost van Uffelen 15r, Christopher
Wood 23br, Lara Zanarini 6, Erik Zandboer 5.

Library of Congress Cataloging-in-Publication Data

Spilsbury, Louise, author.
  Superstar mammals / by Louise Spilsbury.
     pages cm. — (Nature's got talent)
  Includes index.
  ISBN 978-1-4777-7052-8 (library binding) — ISBN 978-1-4777-7053-5 (pbk.) —
  ISBN 978-1-4777-7054-2 (6-pack)
  1. Mammals—Juvenile literature. I. Title.
  QL706.2.S65 2015
  599—dc23
                                    2013048505

Manufactured in the United States of America

CPSIA Compliance Information: Batch #WS14PK7: For Further Information contact Rosen Publishing, New York, New York at 1-800-237-9932

Contents

Mammals

There are over 5,000 different types of **mammal** in the world, and they are all amazing in their own way. Mammals come in a huge range of shapes and sizes. They live on land, in the sea, in the sky, and under the ground. In spite of their differences, all mammals have some things in common.

All mammals produce milk to feed their babies and most look after their young until they can survive on their own.

All mammals have a backbone, or spine.

Bats are the only mammals that can fly.

Mammal Superstars

All mammals are amazing, but some are more astonishing than others! In this book we are going to find out about some of the world's most talented mammal superstars.

All mammals are warm-blooded, which means they can control their body temperature, by warming up or cooling down, when necessary.

Secret Stars

Humans are one of the most successful mammals on Earth. We are not as strong, fast, or large as many other mammals. We cannot fly or dive deep under water by ourselves. However, our well-developed brains help us build tools and machines that allow us to fly, dive, move quickly, and much, much more!

Cheetah

The cheetah is a champion sprinter. This beautiful cat takes the medal for being the fastest animal on land. It can run 328 feet (100 m) in just 3.2 seconds. That is three times faster than the fastest human athlete on Earth!

The cheetah's long, heavy tail helps it balance and steer when it makes fast turns at high speed.

Spotting Prey

Cheetahs have fantastic eyesight so they can see animals such as antelopes and hares across wide, open **grasslands**. A cheetah can sprint quickly only for short distances, so it sneaks up on **prey** before attacking.

A cheetah's spotted coat helps it blend in with dry grass.

A flexible spine and long legs help the cheetah take huge strides as it runs. This incredible cat runs so fast, it appears to glide above the ground!

A cheetah's sharp claws grip the ground like the spikes on a sprinter's shoes.

Secret Stars

The pronghorn is the second-fastest land mammal in the world. It can run at more than 53 miles (86 km) per hour, to escape the hungry coyotes and bobcats that chase it. Pronghorns are named for their two-pointed horns, which can grow up to 1 foot (30 cm) long.

Tarsier

Tarsiers are furry bundles of talent. These amazing creatures can sing love songs, jump 40 times their own body length, and swivel their heads 180 degrees. They are also, possibly, one of the cutest-looking creatures on Earth! Let's take a look at some of this star attraction's talents.

A tarsier can flatten and roll its ears back, then roll them out again. Cool!

The tarsier is born with fur and its eyes open. It can climb trees within one hour of birth.

The animal has long hind legs, which grow to twice its head and body length.

8

Eye Can See You!

For their body size and weight, tarsiers have the largest eyes of any mammal. The tarsier has such large eyes because it is a **nocturnal** hunter. Its huge eyes take in any available light in the darkness, which helps the creature to find its prey at night.

The pupils of the tarsier grow bigger to adjust to light in darkness, and shrink to tiny pinholes in daylight.

Top Talent

Tarsiers are super sopranos! These gifted creatures love to sing at a very high pitch. In some species of tarsier, the males and females even duet together to sing a love song to their mate.

Dolphin

Dolphins are among the world's most entertaining animal performers. They swim fast and leap out of the water. Dolphins twist and spin in the air, making them acrobatic gold medal winners! Some dolphins can complete 14 mid-air spins in a row.

A dolphin uses its **flippers** to turn, steer, and stop.

A dolphin moves its strong tail up and down to quickly swim upward from deep water.

A dolphin's smooth skin and long, slim snout make it streamlined. This helps it move speedily through water.

10

Top of the Class

Dolphins are also super smart. Some types of dolphin use a unique whistle as a name, to tell other dolphins who they are. Dolphins can even recognize the unique whistle of a dolphin they have not seen for 20 years!

Dolphins communicate with whistles, clicks, and sign language.

Top Talent

Dolphins can hunt even in dark, murky water. They make sounds that bounce off objects and return to the dolphins as echoes. This is called **echolocation**. It tells dolphins the size, shape, and location of fish in deep water where there is no light.

11

Snow Leopard

Beautiful snow leopards are superb long jumpers. These animals live high up in snowy mountains and can jump more than 50 feet (15 m), a distance of more than 10 times their own body length, over ditches or between rocks! Snow leopards leap large distances to pounce on the wild sheep and goats they eat.

Long, very powerful back legs help the animal spring from rock to rock.

The snow leopard's huge, wide paws stop it from sinking into the snow.

Secret Stars

The snow leopard has few long jump rivals. However, as a high jumper it is no contest for another big cat, the mountain lion. The mountain lion is a record-breaking high jumper. From standing, this astonishing cat can spring 22 feet (7 m) into the air!

A snow leopard's tail is almost as long as its body. The tail helps the animal balance as it leaps.

Ghost Cats

Snow leopards are so difficult to see that they are often called mountain ghosts! Their pale fur has gray and black markings, which help the animals blend in with the rocks and snow of the mountains. This makes it difficult for prey animals to see snow leopards.

New Guinea Singing Dog

Listen up, when it comes to singing, this cute canine is top dog! The howling songs of the New Guinea singing dog are a little like bird calls and whale songs. The dog's singing sounds also include yelps, barks, screams, and whines. The talented animal sometimes even joins other wild dogs to form singing bands that howl in harmony!

The singing dog's howls go up and down, as if it is practicing scales!

In a group, one dog will begin to sing and the others then join in, crooning higher or lower notes to create a song.

New Guinea singing dogs use their songs to communicate with each other.

Secret Stars

Humpback whales are also pop idols! Male whales sing songs with repeating themes and melodies, and the songs are among the loudest sounds made by any animal. Whale songs travel great distances across the ocean. They can be heard more than 20 miles (32 km) away and can last up to 20 minutes.

Cool Climber

New Guinea singing dogs have other talents, too. They are far more flexible than other dogs and can climb, run, jump, and pounce like a cat. The dogs can jump between ledges of rock, and they can even climb trees!

Sifaka

These leaping lemurs spring between trees up to 33 feet (10 m) apart. Sifakas also take the prize for the most graceful gliders. The animals glide in an upright position between trees, sailing effortlessly between them. Even though the trees are sometimes covered in hard spikes, the smart sifakas never hurt themselves.

The sifaka stretches its arms when it leaps. The flaps of hairy skin at the base of the arm help the animal glide through the air.

The sifaka's long and extremely powerful back legs help it leap through the air.

Large hands and feet help the sifaka grip branches when it lands.

16

The sifaka is named for the alarm call it makes to warn other sifakas that there is a **predator** on the ground.

Special Sifakas

Sifakas have many special talents. On land, they prance or hop sideways on their back legs, with their arms outstretched for balance. They use the four teeth in their bottom jaws to comb and clean their own and other sifakas' fur. Some sifakas occasionally eat dirt, to help them **digest** the fruit and leaves they eat.

Secret Stars

Is it a bird? Is it a plane? No, it is a flying squirrel! When leaping through the air, flying squirrels stretch out a wide flap of skin between their front and back legs. This forms a parachute that helps the animals glide through the air for long distances.

Giant Anteater

This incredible animal has a record-breaking tongue. It is also one of the strangest looking creatures on the planet! Its tube-shaped head has a tiny, toothless mouth with a narrow tongue that is 2 feet (60 cm) long. The tongue shoots out of the anteater's mouth 150 times per minute, licking up 30,000 ants, termites, and other insects a day!

The anteater's long, thin tongue reaches into nests to catch the ants inside.

The anteater's nose sniffs out ants under the ground as the animal walks.

Killer Claws

Giant anteaters use their large, sharp front claws to break open the hard mud of termite mounds. If a predator tries to catch them, anteaters also use their fearsome claws as weapons. Anteaters have even killed jaguars and cougars while defending themselves against attacks.

To keep their claws sharp, anteaters walk on their fists, with their claws curled up inside their paws.

Top Talent

Although anteaters may not seem particularly streamlined, they are superb swimmers. When the animals need to cross a wide river, they use their legs to paddle across. They use their long snout as a snorkel, to breathe in air as they swim through the water.

Prairie Dog

Although they are as small as guinea pigs, as a group, prairie dogs are impressive diggers. Teams of prairie dogs dig enormous underground burrows called towns. They extend for miles (km) and have hundreds of different entrances. The largest recorded town covered 25,000 square miles (40,233 sq km)!

Brown fur **camouflages** the prairie dog against mud to hide it from predators.

A prairie dog's five-toed feet have sharp, thick black claws for digging.

20

That's Teamwork!

Prairie dogs are successful because they work in teams. While some prairie dogs dig or feed, others keep a lookout for danger from a tree or high mound of dirt. If a predator approaches, the guard dog warns the others to run for cover. The animals also take turns babysitting and caring for young.

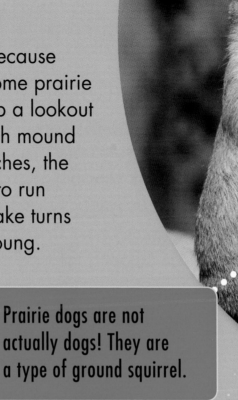

Prairie dogs are not actually dogs! They are a type of ground squirrel.

Top Talent

After humans, prairie dogs have the most advanced language of any mammal. The animals use different sounds as words to describe predators or dangers such as humans, hawks, and coyotes. Scientists believe the animals even have words to describe things such as size and color!

Polar Bear

Long Distance Swimmer

Polar bears are swimming champions. They can swim more than 60 miles (100 km) without resting. Polar bears swim in the freezing waters of the Arctic, where most animals could not survive. The bears swim between floating blocks of ice and land, in search of seals.

The polar bear is kept warm by a thick layer of fat, called blubber, that is 2–4 inches (5–10 cm) thick.

Polar bears use their large front feet to paddle and their back legs to steer.

22

Ice Hunters

Polar bears hunt seals in wide cracks in the sea ice or at holes in the ice where swimming seals come up for air. The bears sneak up on their prey or patiently lie by a seal breathing hole for hours, waiting for a seal to appear.

Little bumps and long hairs on a polar bear's feet stop it from slipping in the snow.

Top Talent

When a polar bear's nose twitches, it means trouble! A polar bear's sense of smell is so powerful it can sense a dead seal on the ice 20 miles (32 km) away, a seal 3 feet (1 m) under snow, and find a seal's air hole in the ice up to 1 mile (1.6 km) away.

23

Red Kangaroo

Red kangaroos are built for bouncing! Of all mammals, they are the fastest jumpers. These kangaroos can jump at speeds of more than 35 miles (56 km) per hour. As the animals bounce along, they make leaps of up to 25 feet (8 m) long and jumps of up to 6 feet (1.8 m) high.

A kangaroo uses its large and powerful back legs and feet to spring into the air.

A kangaroo cannot move its legs one after the other, like a human. Instead, it hops by pushing both feet off the ground at the same time.

A long, thick, strong tail helps the kangaroo balance and turn when it is hopping about. The animal also sits back on its tail for support when it rests.

Boxing Champions

Red kangaroos are boxing champions. Male red kangaroos fight each other, and predators, by biting, kicking, and boxing. They punch enemies with their front paws. They grab the animal with their claws while leaning back on their tail, then they bounce forward to kick it with their huge back feet.

Secret Stars

The kangaroo rat is so-called because it has large back legs and can jump high, like a kangaroo. In fact, for their size, kangaroo rats are the longest jumpers of any mammal. They can leap as far as 6.6 feet (2 m) in one hop. That is almost 45 times their own body length!

25

Blue Whale

This gentle giant is simply the largest animal that has ever lived. The blue whale is as big as a jumbo jet! It weighs around 150 tons (136 t), which is about the same weight as 150 cars. The whale can grow up to 98 feet (30 m) long, that is as long as eight cars parked end-to-end!

Heavyweight Champion

The heart of a blue whale is the size of a small car.

A blue whale's blood vessels are big enough for a human to swim through.

Secret Stars

Even baby blue whales are supersized. When they are born, baby blue whales are already the weight of two cars. As they drink their mothers' rich milk, the babies put on even more weight. In fact, they gain an extra 200 pounds (91 kg) each day of their first year.

When a blue whale comes to the surface to breathe, the spray from its blowhole can reach almost 30 feet (9 m) into the air.

Big Eater, Tiny Food

The biggest animal in the world eats one of the smallest! Blue whales eat krill, a tiny shrimp-like creature. Blue whales have long, bristly plates, called baleen, in their mouths. Like a sieve, baleen strain krill from the water swallowed by the whale.

An adult blue whale may eat as much as 8 tons (7.2 t) of krill in one day!

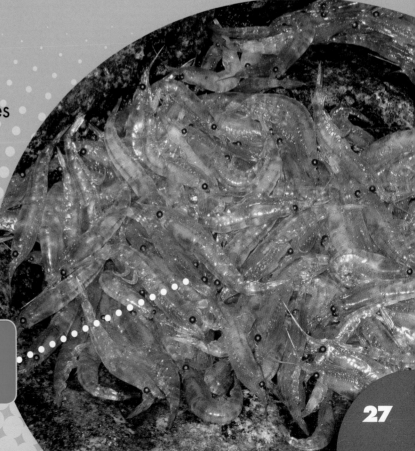

Amazing Adaptations

Some animals are superstars because they have developed body features to help them survive. This is called physical **adaptation**. For example, the polar bear has developed fur that looks white so prey cannot see it in the snow.

A jack rabbit's huge ears are an adaptation. The ears are covered in tiny blood vessels. When blood passes through the ears, heat is given off to stop the rabbit from overheating.

Behavioral Adaptations

Some adaptations are behavioral. These are things that all animals do to survive. For example, some mammals survive cold winters by **hibernating**. They sleep somewhere warm until spring. Snow monkeys sit in warm water to keep warm, and wild hamsters avoid the heat of the day in the desert by coming out only at night. Their behavioral adaptations are one of the many features that make mammals some of nature's superstars.

When it is cold, Japanese snow monkeys adapt by sitting in the warm water of mountain springs.

Top Talent

Migration is one of the most impressive of mammal adaptations. To give birth to young, humpback whales make a migration of 5,280 miles (8,500 km) each way between Antarctica and warm seas. Each year, more than 2 million wildebeest cross miles (km) of land to find grass to eat.

Glossary

adaptation (a-dap-TAY-shun) A feature or way of behaving that helps an animal survive.

camouflages (KA-muh-flahj-ez) When the natural coloring or shape of an animal allows it to blend in with its surroundings.

digest (dy-JEST) To break down food within the body.

echolocation (eh-koh-loh-KAY-shun) Sending out sounds which then bounce off objects and return to the sender as echoes.

flippers (FLIH-perz) Limbs on the body of a marine animal, such as a dolphin. Flippers are used for swimming.

grasslands (GRAS-landz) Large areas of grass with few trees and bushes.

hibernating (HY-bur-nayt-ing) Sleeping through the winter as a way of conserving energy and surviving extreme cold.

mammal (MA-mul) An animal that has live young and that feeds its offspring with milk from its body.

migration (my-GRAY-shun) To travel across a large distance in search of food or warmer conditions, or to return to breeding grounds.

nocturnal (nok-TUR-nul) To sleep during the day and be active during the night.

predator (PREH-duh-tur) An animal that hunts and eats other animals.

prey (PRAY) An animal that is hunted and eaten by other animals.

Further Reading

Inserra, Rose. *Mammals.* Weird, Wild, and Wonderful. New York: Gareth Stevens Learning Library, 2010.

Kaspar, Anna. *What's a Mammal?* All About Animals. New York: PowerKids Press, 2012.

Koontz, Robin Michal. *Screams and Songs: How Animals Communicate to Survive.* Amazing Animal Skills. New York: Cavendish Square Publishing, 2012.

Websites

Due to the changing nature of Internet links, PowerKids Press has developed an online list of websites related to the subject of this book. This site is updated regularly. Please use this link to access the list:
www.powerkidslinks.com/ngt/mamm/

Index